# Ce... America

## A Guide to America's Greatest Symbols

PICTURE WINDOW BOOKS
a capstone imprint

# Celebrate America

## A Guide to America's Greatest Symbols

# Flag Facts

∂∂ The U.S. flag has many nicknames. Some people call it the Stars and Stripes. Others call it the Star-Spangled Banner, Old Glory, and the Red, White, and Blue.

The U.S. Flag

∂∂ Today, the Fort McHenry flag rests in the Smithsonian Institution, in Washington, D.C. A curtain protects it from light and dust. Visitors can view the flag for only a few moments once every hour, when the curtain is pulled back.

∂∂ On August 3, 1949, President Harry S. Truman made June 14 National Flag Day.

The flag that floated over Fort McHenry

∂∂ Vexillology (vek-seh-LAH-leh-jee) is the study of flags. Someone who knows a lot about flags is called a vexillologist (vek-seh-LAH-leh-jist).

Harry S. Truman

# The Liberty Bell

Welcome to the Liberty Bell!
I'm Clara, a tour guide at
the Liberty Bell Center
in Philadelphia, Pennsylvania.

# What Is the Liberty Bell?

The Liberty Bell is a famous symbol of freedom. The bell was made when Great Britain still ruled over the American Colonies. In 1776, colonists rang the bell when they decided to break free of British rule. Are you wondering how the Liberty Bell got cracked? Read on to find out!

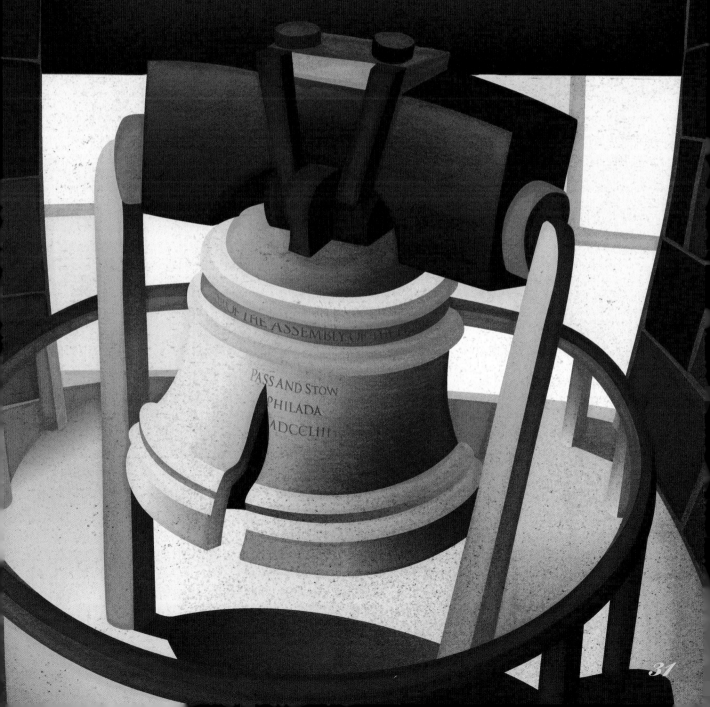

## A Call to Gather

Early American settlers needed a way to announce important events. The best way was by ringing a bell. The toll of the bell would bring people to their town square to find out what was going on.

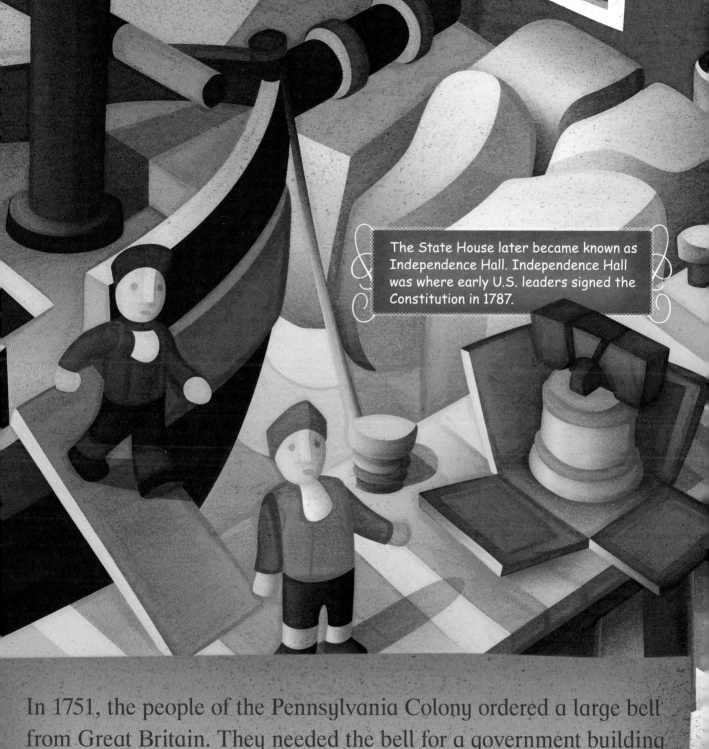

The State House later became known as Independence Hall. Independence Hall was where early U.S. leaders signed the Constitution in 1787.

In 1751, the people of the Pennsylvania Colony ordered a large bell from Great Britain. They needed the bell for a government building in Philadelphia. The building was called the State House.

The bell was tested after it arrived. The people in Philadelphia found the bell was cracked.

# The Bell Makers

John Pass and John Stow were given the job of making a better bell. The men were founders. A founder is a person who makes things out of metal. Pass and Stow melted the bell from Great Britain and added new metals to it.

The Liberty Bell is made mostly of copper and tin. It also includes small amounts of other metals, such as lead, zinc, silver, gold, and nickel.

In March 1753, the colonists tested the new bell, but they still didn't like the sound it made. Pass and Stow melted the bell again and made yet another new bell. Leaders in Philadelphia decided to keep Pass and Stow's second bell. It became the official State House bell.

# Ring of Freedom

The bell at the State House rang often. Its sound called citizens together for special events. On July 8, 1776, the bell rang to announce very important news. The bell's toll that day called people to hear the first reading of the Declaration of Independence.

Leaders from the 13 American Colonies passed the Declaration of Independence on July 4, 1776. The leaders met at the State House in Philadelphia.

## Keeping It Safe

During the Revolutionary War, battles against the British broke out in Philadelphia. In 1777, the bell was moved to the village of Allentown, Pennsylvania, and hidden under the floor of a church. When the British left Philadelphia in 1778, the bell was returned to the State House. From 1790 to 1800, Philadelphia was the capital of the United States.

Many bells were hidden during the Revolutionary War. This prevented the British from melting them and using the metal to make cannons.

39

The name "Liberty Bell" was first used in 1835.

## Who Named the Bell?

The Liberty Bell has a message of freedom written on it. It says, "Proclaim Liberty throughout all the land unto all the inhabitants thereof." These words mean that all Americans should be free.

In the 1830s, many people in the United States wanted to end slavery. These people believed Americans should be free no matter the color of their skin. They began using the bell as a symbol of their beliefs.

They printed drawings of the bell in their newspapers and pamphlets. One such pamphlet included a poem called "The Liberty Bell." The State House bell was soon known by this new name.

# A Final Ring

Each year, the bell rang out to celebrate the birthday of George Washington. The country's first president was born on February 22. On that date, Americans celebrated his birth and his great deeds.

Something went wrong on Washington's birthday in 1846. People in Philadelphia rang the Liberty Bell many times that day. Finally, a strange sound came out. A small crack in the metal had grown longer. The bell would never ring loudly again.

In 1852, the Liberty Bell was removed from the State House steeple. The bell was then put on display inside the building.

## The Bell Travels

Slavery ended in the United States in 1865. The Civil War had been won by the North, and all of the slaves were freed. Soon, the Liberty Bell took on a new meaning. It was used to help bring people in the North and South together again.

The Liberty Bell was taken to cities across the country. It was displayed in New Orleans, Chicago, Atlanta, and other places. It helped all Americans remember the history they shared.

The last time the Liberty Bell left Philadelphia was in 1915. The bell was taken to San Francisco for display at a huge fair.

## Celebrating Freedom

In 1976, the United States had its bicentennial. That meant 200 years had passed since the Colonies broke free from Great Britain.

A building called the Liberty Bell Pavilion was built for the celebration.

The bell was taken out of the State House, which had become known as Independence Hall, and was hung in the new pavilion. The new building made it easier for crowds of people to see the bell.

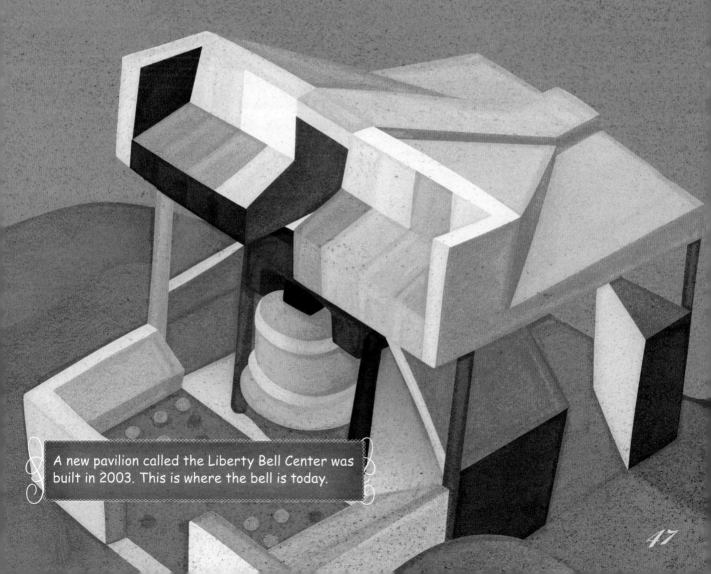

A new pavilion called the Liberty Bell Center was built in 2003. This is where the bell is today.

47

The Liberty Bell is part of the Independence National Historical Park. You can see the Liberty Bell anytime, day or night. It's enclosed in glass and is always visible. Goodbye and thank you for visiting!

# Liberty Bell Facts

∞  Pennsylvania Colony paid about $300 in today's dollars for the first State House bell.

∞  The Liberty Bell has a yoke made of a special wood called slippery elm or American elm. The bell weighs 2,080 pounds (936 kilograms).

∞  The bell's metal is 3 inches (7.6 centimeters) thick at the bottom of the bell.

∞  The bottom of the bell measures 12 feet (3.7 meters) around.

The Liberty Bell

The Pennsylvania Colony

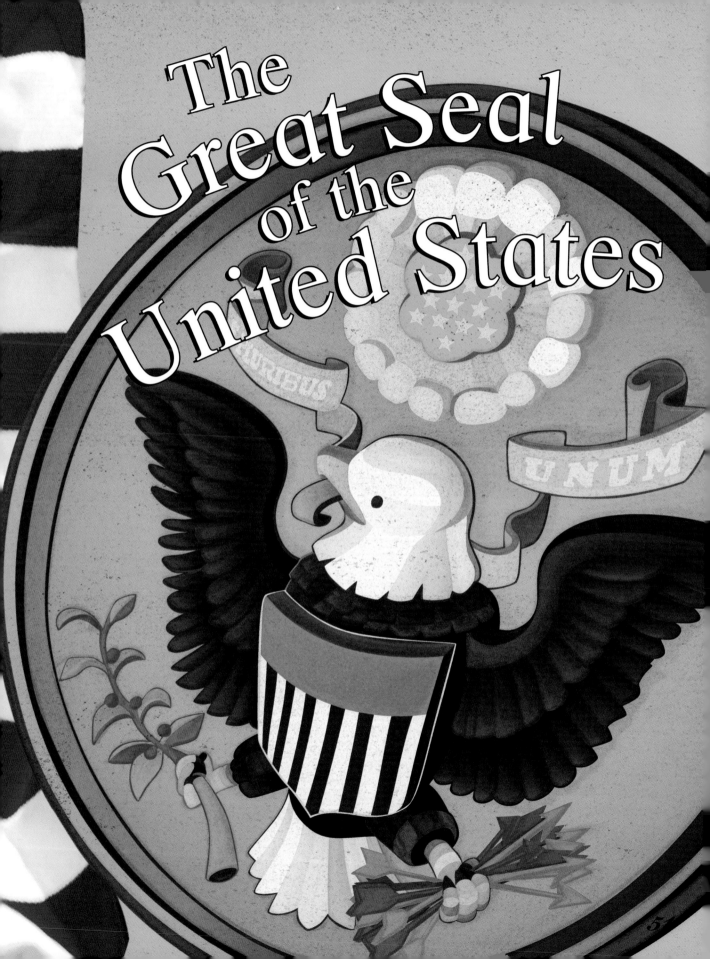

# The Great Seal of the United States

My name is Benjamin Franklin.
I helped make the first laws of the United
States more than 200 years ago. I also
helped design the Great Seal. The
Great Seal is a symbol of the
United States and the U.S.
government. Let me tell
you more about it!

## What Is the Great Seal?

The Great Seal is a special mark. It is put on important government papers. People know that any paper with the Great Seal on it is from the U.S. government.

No one except the U.S. government is allowed to use the Great Seal.

# A Country Is Born

The story of the Great Seal starts on July 4, 1776. That's when the Declaration of Independence was approved, and the United States of America was born.

The new country needed to set itself apart from other countries. The United States needed its own seal. A committee was formed to design one.

First Committee

## Three Committees, Three Designs

The first design committee included Thomas Jefferson, John Adams, and me, Benjamin Franklin. We all had different ideas about what the seal should look like.

Congress had its own ideas, too. During the next six years, two more committees tried to create a seal. No one could find the perfect design.

Second Committee

Third Committee

Thomas Jefferson and John Adams had a lot in common. Both loved their country. Both signed the Declaration of Independence. Both later became President of the United States. And both died on July 4, 1826.

## The Finished Product

Congress decided to give the seal project to Charles Thomson, the Secretary of Congress. Thomson looked at the ideas of all three committees. He asked a lawyer named William Barton to help him put the ideas together. Just seven days later, on June 20, 1782, Congress approved their design.

In 1782, seals were two-sided wax disks. They had one design on the front and one on the back. Later, seals were pressed into paper. Only the front design appeared. Today, only the front of the Great Seal is pressed into important U.S. government papers.

## The Great Seal's Front

All of the objects and words on the Great Seal of the United States mean something. Do you see the bald eagle on the front? Thomson and Barton chose a North American bird because the seal is a symbol of a North American country.

The eagle has a shield with 13 red and white stripes. The number 13 appears many times on the Great Seal. It stands for the first 13 states of the United States. Above the stripes is a blue band. It stands for Congress.

The eagle has a ribbon in its beak. On the ribbon are the Latin words *E Pluribus Unum*. In English, these words mean "out of many, one." The words say that the many U.S. states came together as one strong country.

The eagle holds an olive branch in one claw. The branch is a symbol of peace. In its other claw, the eagle holds 13 arrows. The arrows show that Americans will fight to stay free.

Above the eagle are 13 stars in a ring of light. The stars stand for the United States taking its place among the other great countries of the world.

# The Great Seal's Back

On the back of the Great Seal is an unfinished pyramid. It has 13 steps. The pyramid is a symbol of the United States' long-lasting strength.

The eye is called the Eye of Providence. Above it are the Latin words *Annuit Coeptis*. In English, these words mean "He [God] has favored our undertakings." Together, the eye and the words suggest that the United States has a bright future.

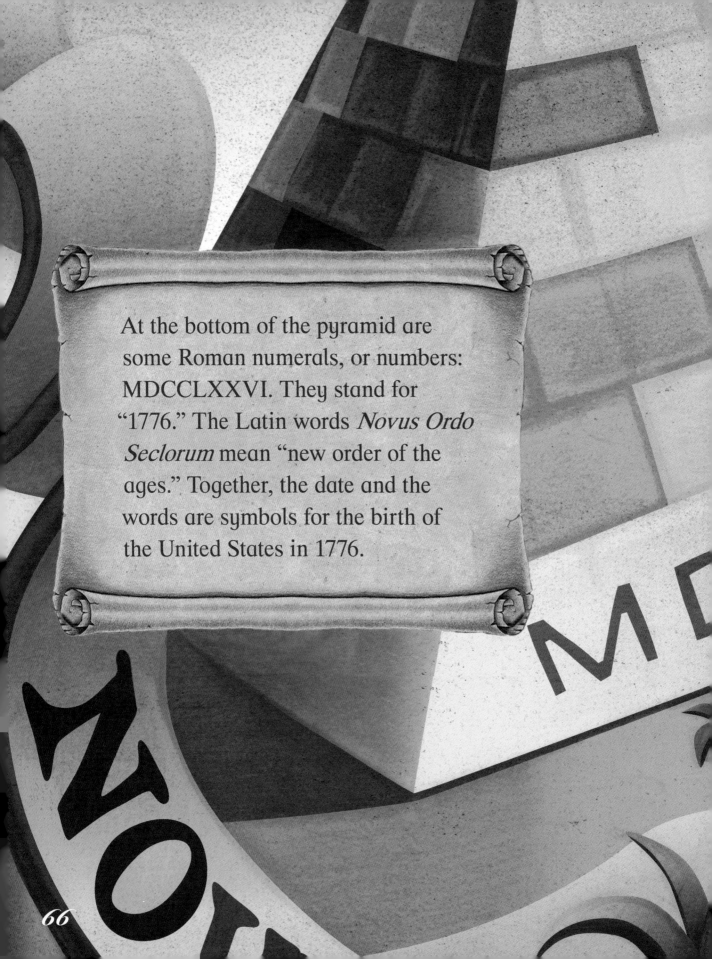

At the bottom of the pyramid are some Roman numerals, or numbers: MDCCLXXVI. They stand for "1776." The Latin words *Novus Ordo Seclorum* mean "new order of the ages." Together, the date and the words are symbols for the birth of the United States in 1776.

CCLXXVI

The front and back designs of the Great Seal are on the back of the $1 bill.

## Seeing the Great Seal

The Great Seal appears on many important U.S. government papers. For example, the Great Seal is put on treaties. Treaties are agreements with other countries.

The tool used to press the Great Seal into government papers is in Washington, D.C. It sits in the Exhibit Hall of the State Department. Because the Great Seal is a valued symbol of the United States, this tool is well guarded.

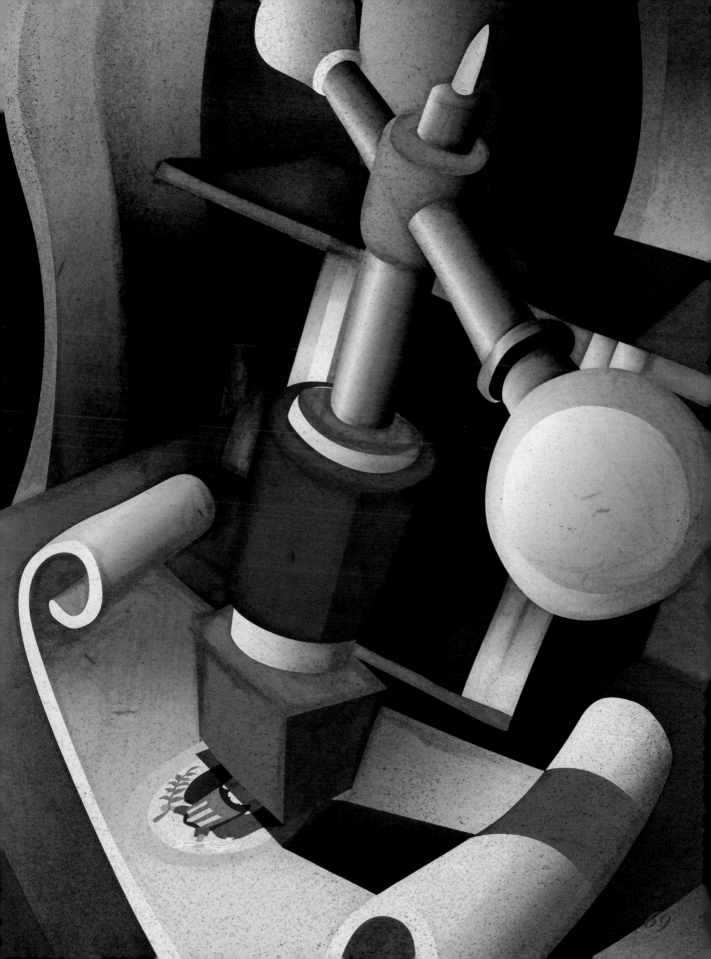

Now you know the story of the Great Seal of the United States. Look for the seal the next time someone gives you a dollar bill. See if you can find all of the symbols you just read about!

# Great Seal Facts

❧   Kings and other rulers have used seals for more than 6,000 years.

❧   Charles Thomson did not show any artwork to Congress. Members approved his design for the Great Seal from a written description.

❧   The bald eagle is not really bald. It has white feathers on its head. *Bald* is an old word for "white."

❧   The Great Seal is used on important U.S. government papers between 2,000 and 3,000 times a year.

❧   The Secretary of State is in charge of the Great Seal. Thomas Jefferson was the first Secretary of State of the United States and the first to take on this duty.

Thomas Jefferson

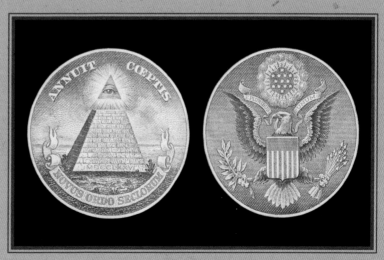

The Great Seal

Uncle Sam

I WANT YOU FOR U.S. ARMY
NEAREST RECRUITING STATION

My name is Sam Wilson. I may not look familiar to you. But you may have heard my nickname before—Uncle Sam. I'm a symbol of the U.S. government.

How did I become Uncle Sam? It happened because of cartoons, a circus clown, and millions of posters.

Here's my story.

## A Pair of Initials

During the War of 1812, my brother and I were meatpackers. We packed meat in wooden barrels. The U.S. government then sent the barrels to the soldiers. Each barrel was marked with the letters *U.S.*, which stood for "United States."

Some soldiers thought *U.S.* stood for me, Sam Wilson, or "Uncle Sam." Soon the name Uncle Sam became a nickname for the government of the United States.

The United States and Uncle Sam have the same initials, U.S.

# A Cartoon Character

In the early days of the United States, many magazines and newspapers had cartoons. The drawings focused on world events. Cartoonists wanted a character to stand for the United States.

WHO'S ABSENT?

Is it YOU?

English cartoonists used a character named John Bull to stand for their country. He wore a vest with an English flag on it.

## Stars and Stripes

For years, U.S. cartoonists drew characters wearing stars and stripes. They drew Yankee Doodle. They drew Brother Jonathan, a character who was said to be named after Governor Jonathan Trumbull of Connecticut. Both of these characters were created during the Revolutionary War (1775–1783).

Brother Jonathan

Yankee Doodle

Brother Jonathan

# Uncle Sam

As the country grew, cartoonists created another character to symbolize the United States. They named him Uncle Sam. At first, Uncle Sam looked like Brother Jonathan. The two characters wore the same clothes: a top hat, a long coat with tails, and striped pants.

# A Famous Clown

In the mid-1800s, some cartoonists started modeling Uncle Sam after a famous clown. The clown's name was Dan Rice. He wore red, white, and blue costumes.

By the 1860s, Dan Rice was so popular that he made more money per year than President Abraham Lincoln.

## Looking Like a President

After the Civil War (1861–1865), a cartoonist named Thomas Nast gave Uncle Sam a new look. He made Uncle Sam look a little like President Abraham Lincoln. He drew a tall, thin man with a beard. Other cartoonists did the same.

87

## Birthday Presents

In 1876, the United States turned 100 years old. To celebrate the country's birthday, people made and sold gifts of all kinds. Many items had pictures of Uncle Sam on them.

Songs were also written about Uncle Sam, including "Uncle Sam's Farm."

# I Want You

One more artist had a say in how Uncle Sam looked. In 1916, James Montgomery Flagg drew himself as Uncle Sam. His drawing was on the cover of a magazine. Then it was printed on a U.S. Army poster. The poster urged people to join the Army during World War I (1914–1918).

The United States entered World War I in 1917, and the need for soldiers was great. More than 4 million copies of the "I Want You" poster were made between 1917 and 1918.

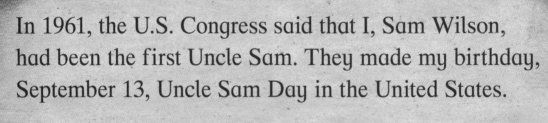

In 1961, the U.S. Congress said that I, Sam Wilson, had been the first Uncle Sam. They made my birthday, September 13, Uncle Sam Day in the United States.

That's the story of one of our country's most recognized symbols. I hope you enjoyed it!

# Uncle Sam Facts

Sam Wilson, the original Uncle Sam, was born in Arlington, Massachusetts, in 1766. He spent most of his life in Troy, New York, where he died in 1854.

Before Uncle Sam, Brother Jonathan was a symbol of the United States. Brother Jonathan stood for a strong U.S. government but even stronger separate but equal states. Uncle Sam, on the other hand, stood for strong states but an even stronger U.S. government.

James Montgomery Flagg was a gifted artist long before he drew Uncle Sam. He sold his first illustration at the age of 12. By age 15, he was working for two top magazine publishers.

Uncle Sam poster

James Montgomery Flagg

93

94

# The White House

My name is Keneesha.
I'm a White House Secret Service agent. I'm here to show you the most famous house in the country—the home and office of the president of the United States.

The White House welcomes about 1,000 visitors every day!

# The White House

The White House is an important symbol of leadership and democracy. It is where some of the most important decisions about the United States are made.

97

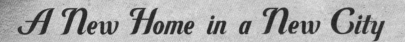

# A New Home in a New City

George Washington picked the place for the White House in 1790. He chose a wooded area near the Potomac River.

The White House was part of a large project: to build a city for the U.S. government. That city became known as Washington, D.C.

## Who Designed It?

The president's house had to be special. A contest was held to see who had the best design.

An Irishman named James Hoban won. His building looked a lot like Leinster House, a government building in Dublin, Ireland.

The first name for the White House was the President's House. It was later named the Executive Mansion. In 1901, President Theodore Roosevelt officially changed its name to the White House.

## The First Family Moves In

The first president to live in the White House was John Adams, the second president of the United States. He moved in with his family in 1800, but the White House wasn't finished yet. There were no water pipes. The rooms had no heat. There was no place to dry the family's laundry. President Adams' wife, Abigail, had to hang clothes on ropes in the East Room!

The first president of the United States, George Washington, never lived in the White House. He was the only president who didn't live there.

# Wartime and the White House

President James Madison and his wife, Dolley, moved into the White House in 1809. Sadly, during the War of 1812, the British burned the building. Only the outside walls survived the fire. After the war ended, the U.S. government rebuilt the White House on the site of the ruins. In 1817, the new president, James Monroe, moved in.

# Growing Pains

Over the years, the White House changed many times, and in many different ways. The United States was growing, and so was the president's staff.

White House workers needed more space. More rooms, floors, the East Wing, and the West Wing were added to the building.

President Theodore Roosevelt and his family moved into the White House in 1901. They brought along all sorts of pets, including a parrot, a snake, and a pony named Algonquin, who actually rode in the White House elevator.

# The Oval Office

The Oval Office is the president's office. The egg-shaped room was finished in 1909, when William Howard Taft was president. Every president since then has redecorated the office to suit his or her tastes. The Oval Office is in the West Wing, along with the Cabinet Room and the Situation Room. The West Wing is not open to visitors.

The original Oval Office was destroyed by fire in 1929. Workers built a new Oval Office in 1934 for President Franklin Delano Roosevelt. His office is the one used by today's president.

# The Second Floor

The president and his or her family live on the second floor of the White House. This is also where the president's guests sleep when they spend the night. Overnight guests may sleep in the Rose Room or the Lincoln Bedroom.

## Colored Rooms

President Abraham Lincoln never used the Lincoln Bedroom as a bedroom. When he was president, the room was his office. The room didn't become a bedroom until 1902, 37 years after Lincoln's death.

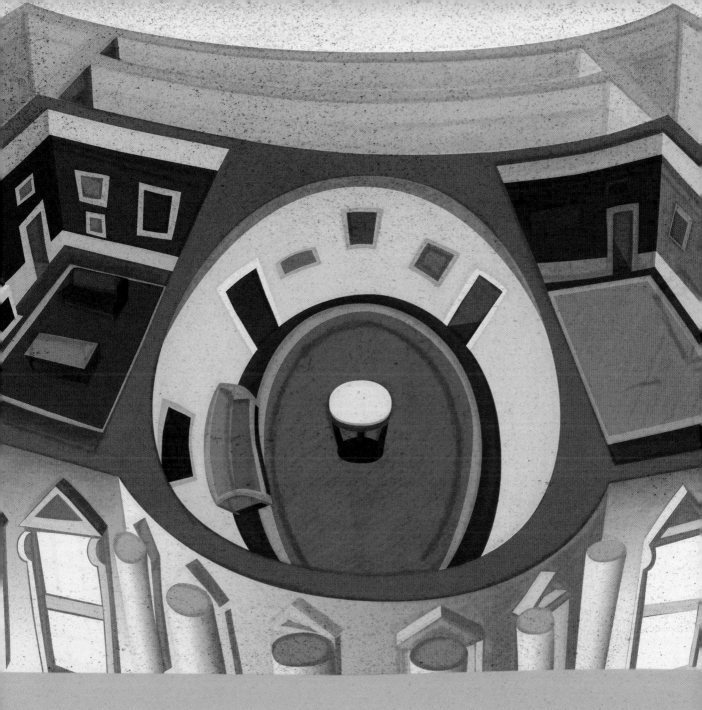

The White House is full of color! The Red Room, the Blue Room, and the Green Room are rooms where the president meets foreign leaders and other important guests.

# The Ground Floor Corridor

Corridors are hallways. They lead from one part of the White House to another. From the Ground Floor Corridor, visitors can peek into the oval-shaped Diplomatic Reception Room. This is where the president welcomes ambassadors, kings, and queens.

# The State Dining Room

The president and the first lady or first gentleman have dinner parties in the State Dining Room. As many as 140 guests can eat here at the same time.

I hope you enjoyed learning about the White House. If you'd like to come see us, call or write a congressman or congresswoman from your state. He or she may be able to send you tickets for a White House tour!

# White House Facts

The original White House took eight years to build and cost about $230,000.

The White House is made of white-painted sandstone.

It takes 570 gallons (2,166 liters) of paint to cover the outside walls of the White House.

Did you know that the White House is much bigger than it looks? A lot of it is below ground or hidden by trees. It has:

— 6 stories
— 412 doors
— 147 windows
— 28 fireplaces
— 8 staircases
— 132 rooms and 35 bathrooms
— a tennis court
— a bowling lane
— a movie theater
— a jogging track
— a swimming pool

The White House

# Our U.S. Capitol

Welcome to our U.S. Capitol! My name is Celine, and I'm a tour guide here. Our U.S. Capitol has become one of the best-known symbols of freedom and democracy in the world. Did you know that it took more than 30 years to build the Capitol? Read on to learn more about it.

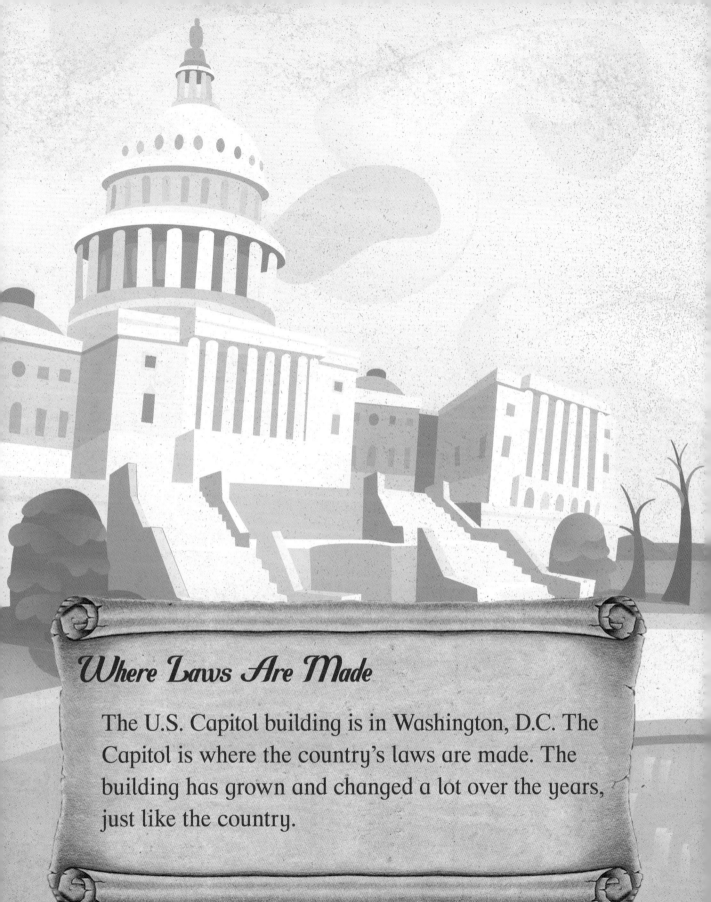

## Where Laws Are Made

The U.S. Capitol building is in Washington, D.C. The Capitol is where the country's laws are made. The building has grown and changed a lot over the years, just like the country.

## The Location

In 1790, leaders of the United States decided on a capital city and named it Washington, after the country's first president, George Washington.

That same year, the U.S. Congress passed a law that said a Capitol building would be built. It would be located on the banks of the Potomac River.

121

## A Winning Idea

Finding someone to design the Capitol building was not easy. Thomas Jefferson, a top government official, suggested having a design contest. The contest promised $500 to the winner. But Washington and Jefferson didn't like any of the 17 ideas entered in the contest.

A doctor named William Thornton sent in his design after the contest was over. Both Washington and Jefferson liked Thornton's ideas the best, so his design was chosen. Construction of the U.S. Capitol building began in 1793.

An architect named James Hoban was hired to watch over Thornton's project. Hoban had designed the White House before he worked on the U.S. Capitol.

# Parts of the Capitol

Thornton's design had a dome and rotunda in the center and large wings, or sections, to the north and south.

The north wing was finished in 1800. It housed the Senate Chamber. In the same wing, the Supreme Court Chamber was completed in 1810.

The south wing was finished in 1807. The House of Representatives met in the House Chamber in the south wing.

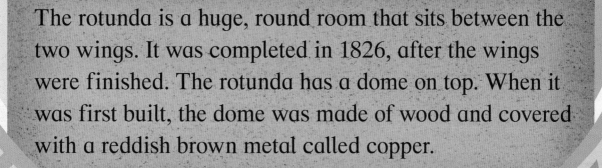

The rotunda is a huge, round room that sits between the two wings. It was completed in 1826, after the wings were finished. The rotunda has a dome on top. When it was first built, the dome was made of wood and covered with a reddish brown metal called copper.

What the dome visitors see today is the result of an addition that was completed in 1863. It features beautiful paintings on the ceiling.

125

# The Capitol During War

The Capitol building was still unfinished when the War of 1812 (1812–1815) broke out. Battles were fought near Washington, and the British set fire to buildings. As the Capitol burned, a rainstorm moved over the city. The rain put out the flames. The Capitol was still standing, but the insides were nearly destroyed.

After surviving the War of 1812 and the fire, the Capitol was finally finished in 1826—33 years after construction had started.

An architect named Benjamin Henry Latrobe had worked on construction of the Capitol. He was given the job of repairing the Capitol after the War of 1812. Later, a man named Charles Bullfinch took over his job and finished the work.

128

## A Growing Nation

The population of the United States almost doubled between 1840 and 1860. New states were added, so more senators and representatives were coming to Washington. Soon the Capitol was too small.

Construction that lasted from 1851 to 1868 doubled the size of the Capitol. Workers added new wings and built new chambers for the House of Representatives and the Senate.

## A Bigger Dome

The new wings made the dome at the center of the building look too small. The old dome was removed, and work began on a new one. The new dome was made of cast iron. The metal made it fireproof.

American artist Thomas Crawford created a huge statue called "Freedom" for the top of the dome. It stood more than 19 feet (5.8 m) tall. "Freedom" was placed on top of the dome in December 1863.

The Capitol's cast iron dome weighs nearly 9 million pounds (4 million kilograms). That's the total weight of about 2,250 cars!

# A Soldiers' Hospital

When the Civil War (1861–1865) began, the construction at the Capitol stopped briefly. President Abraham Lincoln thought that if construction continued, it would be a good sign that the country would make it through the war. Soon, Congress ordered the construction on the wings to restart.

During the war, soldiers lived in the Capitol. The building also served as a hospital for wounded troops. The basement was turned into a bakery so soldiers would have a fresh supply of bread.

Throughout the years, the Capitol has changed to keep up with the times. In the 1850s, the building got indoor plumbing. Electricity was added in the 1880s. Air conditioning was added in 1928.

# A Modern Capitol

In 1962, a very large addition was finished on the east front side of the Capitol. In 1976, the old Senate chamber, National Statuary Hall, and the old Supreme Court chamber were restored. In 1983, the west walls of the Capitol were strengthened and restored.

Throughout the years, the Capitol has gotten its own power plant, subway system, and post office. In some ways, it works like a small city.

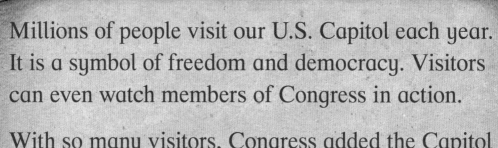

Millions of people visit our U.S. Capitol each year. It is a symbol of freedom and democracy. Visitors can even watch members of Congress in action.

With so many visitors, Congress added the Capitol Visitor Center in 2007 to improve comfort and safety for everyone.

I hope you enjoyed learning about the U.S. Capitol. Come visit soon!

# U.S. Capitol Facts

The Capitol

✎ French architect Pierre L'Enfant was the first man hired to design the Capitol. But he was fired in 1792 because he wouldn't make drawings of his designs. He said he had the plans in his head.

✎ The south wing of the U.S. Capitol holds National Statuary Hall, where statues of successful U.S. citizens are on display. They include former leaders, artists, teachers, and religious figures.

✎ The U.S. flag flies over the House and Senate wings of the Capitol when Congress is in session. At night, a lantern on the top of the dome is also lit, to show that Congress is working.

National Statuary Hall

# The Lincoln Memorial

I'm Phillip, a tour guide at the Lincoln Memorial in Washington, D.C. Because Abraham Lincoln was one of the greatest presidents in U.S. history, the government had a memorial built to honor him. It has become a national symbol of togetherness and freedom. Read on to learn more about President Lincoln and the Lincoln Memorial.

Abraham Lincoln was the 16th president of the United States.

# President Lincoln

Abraham Lincoln led the United States through the Civil War (1861–1865). At the start of the war, some states tried to break away from the United States. Lincoln's army fought to hold the country together. Lincoln also believed slaves should be free. He once said, "If slavery isn't wrong, then nothing is wrong." Lincoln succeeded in winning the Civil War, and the slaves were freed.

# Lincoln Is Shot

President Lincoln was shot in 1865 while watching a play at Ford's Theater in Washington, D.C. He died from his wounds. Lincoln's death was a terrible blow to the country. After his death, Americans began talking about a memorial to honor him and his great deeds.

## A Swampy Site

Years later, Americans took action to honor President Lincoln. In 1911, Congress formed the Lincoln Memorial Commission. Its job was to pick a location for the memorial and find an architect to design it. Henry Bacon was the architect chosen for the job.

In 1902, commissioners picked out land for our nation's memorials and monuments. Swampland was filled in and eventually used for the Lincoln Memorial, the Washington Monument, the Franklin D. Roosevelt Memorial, the Vietnam Memorial, and others.

The commissioners chose Potomac Park in Washington, D.C., for the memorial. The park was a wet, marshy area. Because of all the water, workers had to build a strong platform for the building.

## The Platform

The Lincoln Memorial platform is 14 feet (4.3 meters) high, 257 feet (78.4 m) long, and 187 feet (57 m) wide. Workers spent a full year working on the platform before starting construction on the memorial building.

Work on the Lincoln Memorial began on February 12, 1914. That date would have been Lincoln's 105th birthday.

# The Building

The Lincoln Memorial is made of different types of U.S. marble. It has 36 columns. These columns stand for the number of states that were part of the United States at the time President Lincoln died.

The murals on the walls of the Lincoln Memorial are 12 feet (3.7 m) high and 60 feet (18.3 m) long. That is the length of 10 men lying head to toe!

The memorial is a very large building, but it has only three sections. The center section has a large statue of Abraham Lincoln. The other two sections have walls on which Lincoln's famous speeches were carved by artist Ernest Bairstow. Above the speeches are murals that were painted by Jules Guerin.

The statue of Lincoln is almost as tall as two basketball hoops stacked on top of each other. The statue's head is the size of an armchair. Each thumb is the size of a toaster.

## A Huge Statue

An artist named Daniel Chester French designed the Lincoln statue. French was an American who had studied art in Italy. He first planned to make a statue that was only 10 feet (3.1 m) tall. After meeting with Henry Bacon, the two decided the statue needed to be 19 feet (5.8 m) tall.

# Putting It Together

Although Daniel French designed the statue of Lincoln, he hired Attilio and Furio Piccirilli to carve it. The brothers came from a famous stone-carving family. First, they cut the white marble into 28 pieces. The brothers then went to work carving the statue from the marble pieces. In the end, the statue was put together like a puzzle.

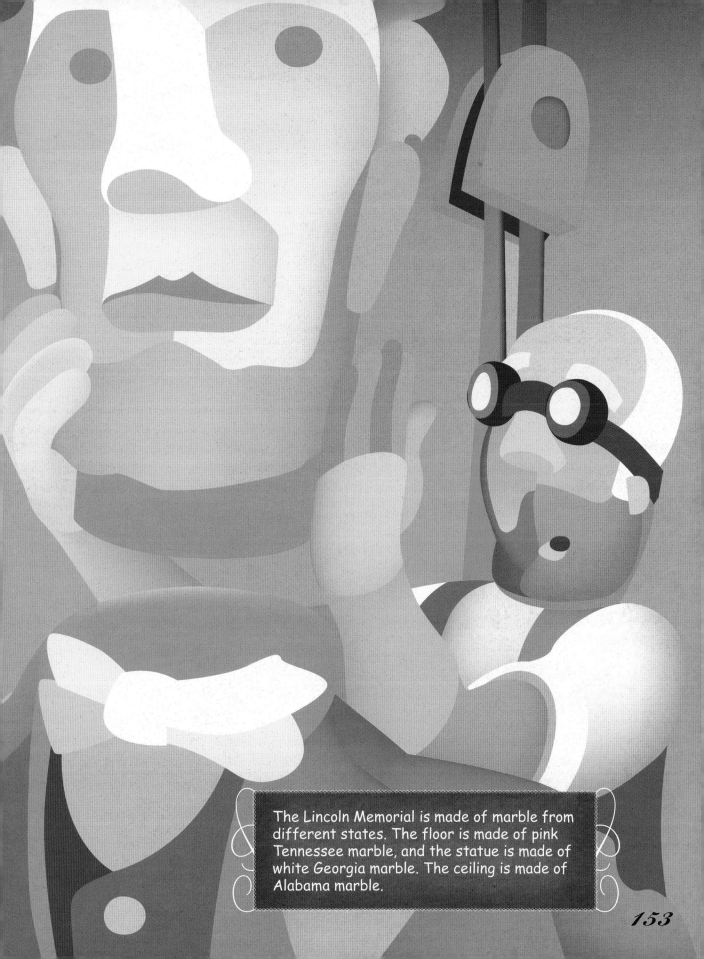

The Lincoln Memorial is made of marble from different states. The floor is made of pink Tennessee marble, and the statue is made of white Georgia marble. The ceiling is made of Alabama marble.

153

154

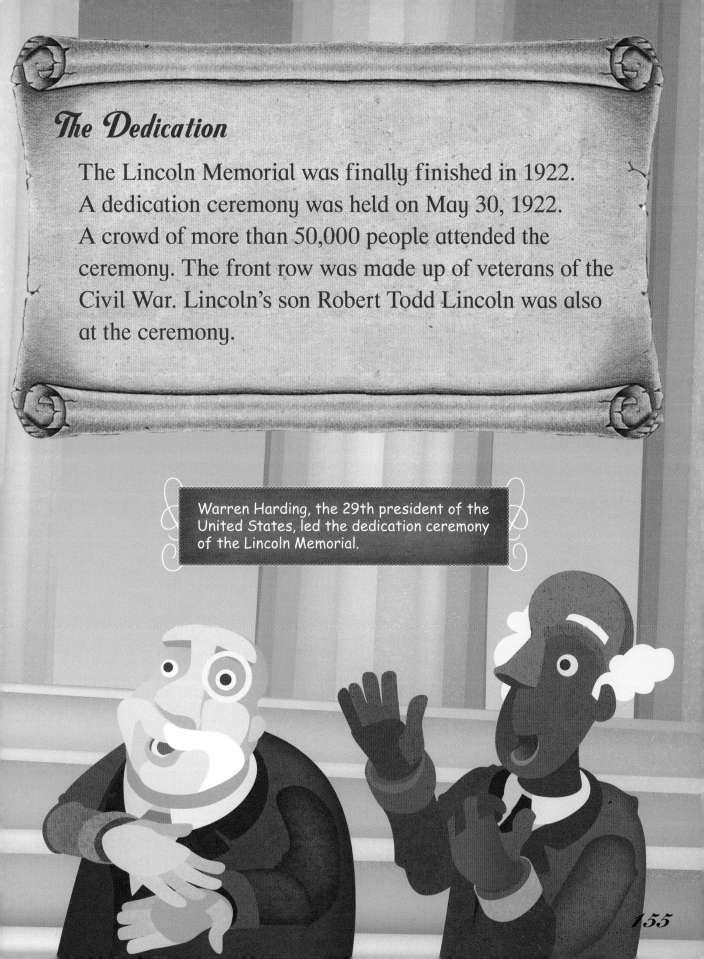

## The Dedication

The Lincoln Memorial was finally finished in 1922. A dedication ceremony was held on May 30, 1922. A crowd of more than 50,000 people attended the ceremony. The front row was made up of veterans of the Civil War. Lincoln's son Robert Todd Lincoln was also at the ceremony.

Warren Harding, the 29th president of the United States, led the dedication ceremony of the Lincoln Memorial.

## A Place for History

Many important events have taken place at the Lincoln Memorial. People have gathered there to hear speeches and singers. They have also gone there to speak out against war and unfairness.

In 1963, Martin Luther King Jr. gave his famous "I Have a Dream" speech on the memorial steps. He called for Americans of all colors to live together in peace.

Marian Anderson, a famous African-American singer, sang at the Lincoln Memorial in 1939. A crowd of 75,000 people showed up for the concert. After Marian sang the last note, the crowd roared its approval and cheered for more.

You can visit the Lincoln Memorial in Washington, D.C. Millions of tourists come to see this American symbol of togetherness and freedom each year. You can explore the building and read Lincoln's famous speeches. I hope you enjoyed learning more about the Lincoln Memorial!

# Lincoln Memorial Facts

꧁ On the statue of Lincoln, his left hand forms a fist. The fist stands for Lincoln's strength. His right hand is open and stands for his kindness.

꧁ The memorial is as tall as a three-story building. The marble stairs in front of the building lead down to a long pool. The Lincoln statue and the columns appear in lights at night. These lights are reflected by the pool.

꧁ During his "I Have a Dream" speech, Martin Luther King Jr. said, "I have a dream that my four little children will one day live in a nation where they will not be judged by the color of their skin but by the content of their character."

The Lincoln Memorial

# The Statue of Liberty

My name is Jeanetta.
I'm a park ranger at Statue of Liberty National Park in New York City. The Statue of Liberty is an important symbol of freedom. Let me tell you her story.

## A Gift from the French

Did you know that the Statue of Liberty was a gift from the people of France? They admired the Colonies' fight for freedom during the Revolutionary War. They wanted to honor the Declaration of Independence. The gift was France's way of saying, "Good job, America!"

French soldiers and sailors fought side-by-side with American troops during the Revolutionary War. Together, they defeated the British and won the war.

# Making the Statue

A French artist named Frederic-Auguste Bartholdi drew up plans for the Statue of Liberty in 1874.

Workers in France used copper sheets for the statue's outside surface, or skin. The sheets were about as thick as two pennies. Workers pounded the copper sheets onto wooden molds.

When the Statue of Liberty was first built, she was reddish brown—the color of new copper. Copper changes color when it's left outside. It turns light green or blue. This change in color is called oxidation.

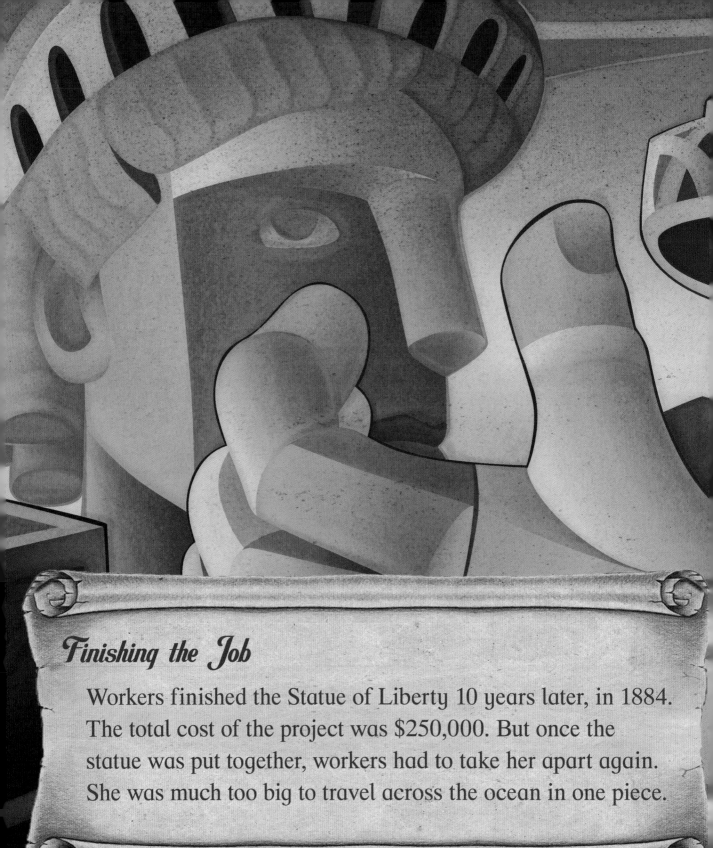

## Finishing the Job

Workers finished the Statue of Liberty 10 years later, in 1884. The total cost of the project was $250,000. But once the statue was put together, workers had to take her apart again. She was much too big to travel across the ocean in one piece.

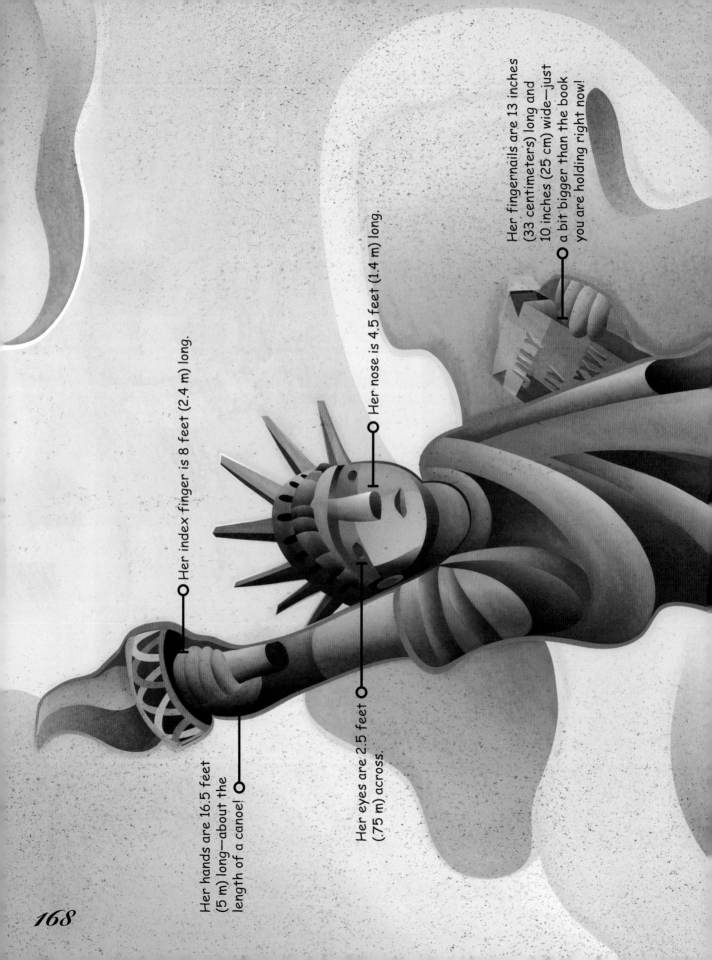

Her index finger is 8 feet (2.4 m) long.

Her nose is 4.5 feet (1.4 m) long.

Her fingernails are 13 inches (33 centimeters) long and 10 inches (25 cm) wide—just a bit bigger than the book you are holding right now!

Her hands are 16.5 feet (5 m) long—about the length of a canoe!

Her eyes are 2.5 feet (.75 m) across.

168

## One Big Statue

How big is the Statue of Liberty? She stands 305 feet (93 meters) tall, from the bottom of the pedestal to the top of the torch. She's about as tall as a 30-story building! That's why workers had to take her apart for her trip from France to the United States.

Her feet are 25 feet (8 m) long.

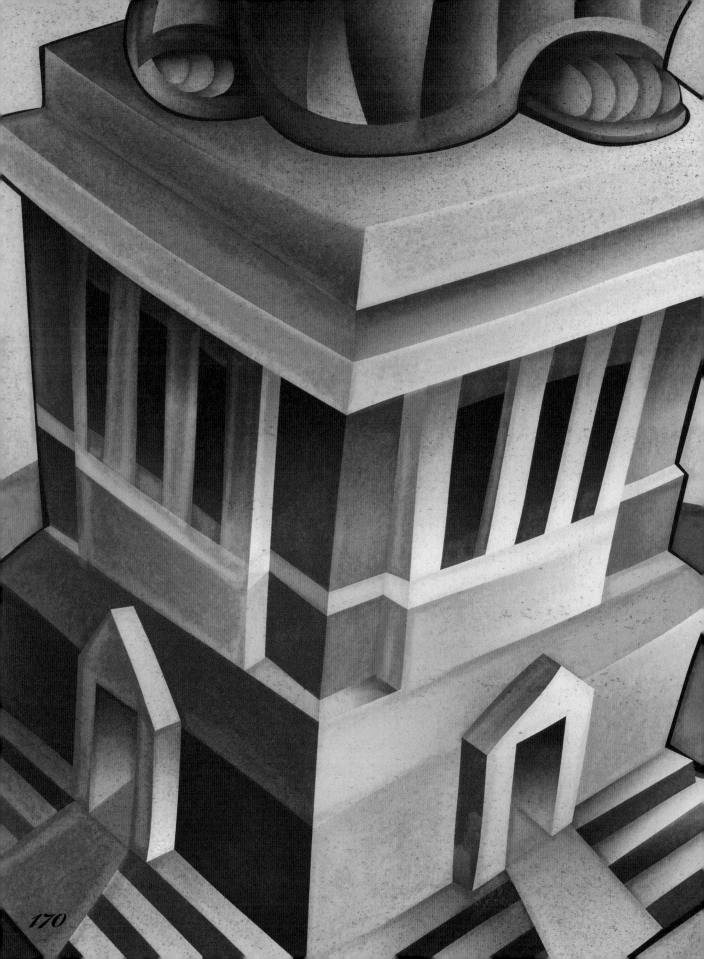

# The Pedestal

French workers built the Statue of Liberty, but U.S. workers built her pedestal. She needed a base to keep her steady in bad weather.

Building the pedestal was going to cost a lot of money. Thankfully, a newspaperman named Joseph Pulitzer helped raise the needed funds. People from all over the United States gave whatever money they could to help the pedestal project.

Pulitzer collected about $100,000 for the pedestal project.

# The Statue Arrives

Packed in boxes, the Statue of Liberty sailed into New York Harbor in June 1885. Her pedestal was finished in April 1886. Workers then spent four months putting her back together.

On October 28, 1886, President Grover Cleveland officially accepted the Statue of Liberty. Thousands of Americans were there to celebrate France's gift.

The Statue of Liberty was packed in 214 different wooden boxes, or crates, for her trip from France to the United States.

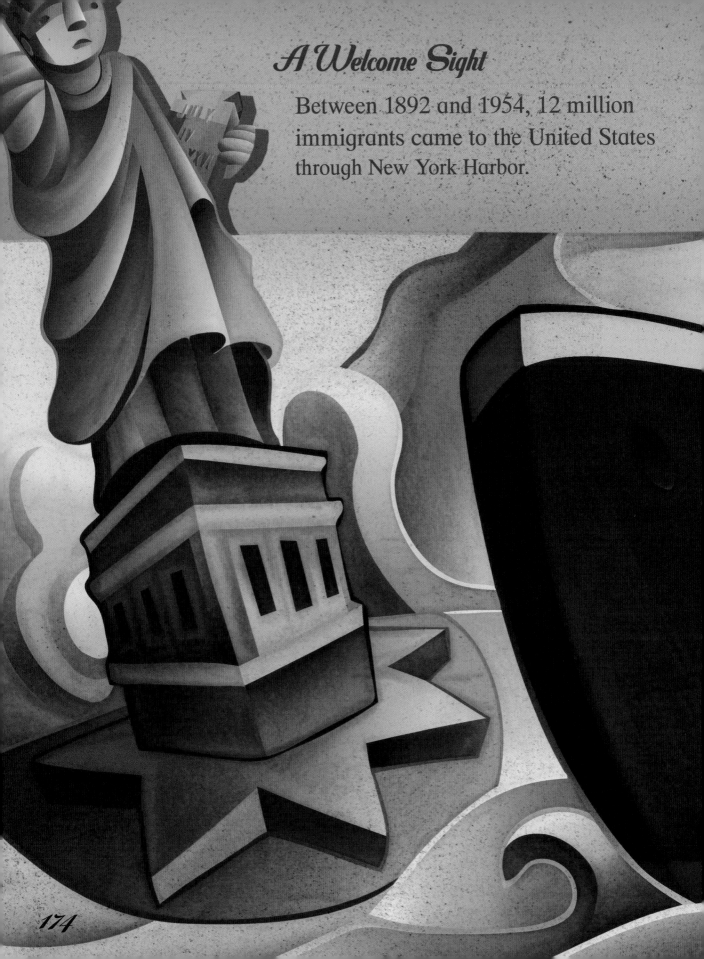

# A Welcome Sight

Between 1892 and 1954, 12 million immigrants came to the United States through New York Harbor.

They came from all over the world on large boats, looking for a new place to live. The Statue of Liberty was one of the first things they saw upon arrival.

Most immigrants who came through New York after 1892 stopped first at Ellis Island. There they were signed in and checked by doctors. Ellis Island lies near the Statue of Liberty.

## A Free Country

Many immigrants came from countries where they could not buy land. Most could not go to school. These rights and many others were only for the rich.

In the United States, almost anyone can own land and go to
school. The Statue of Liberty is a symbol of these freedoms.
She tells the world that the United States is a free country.

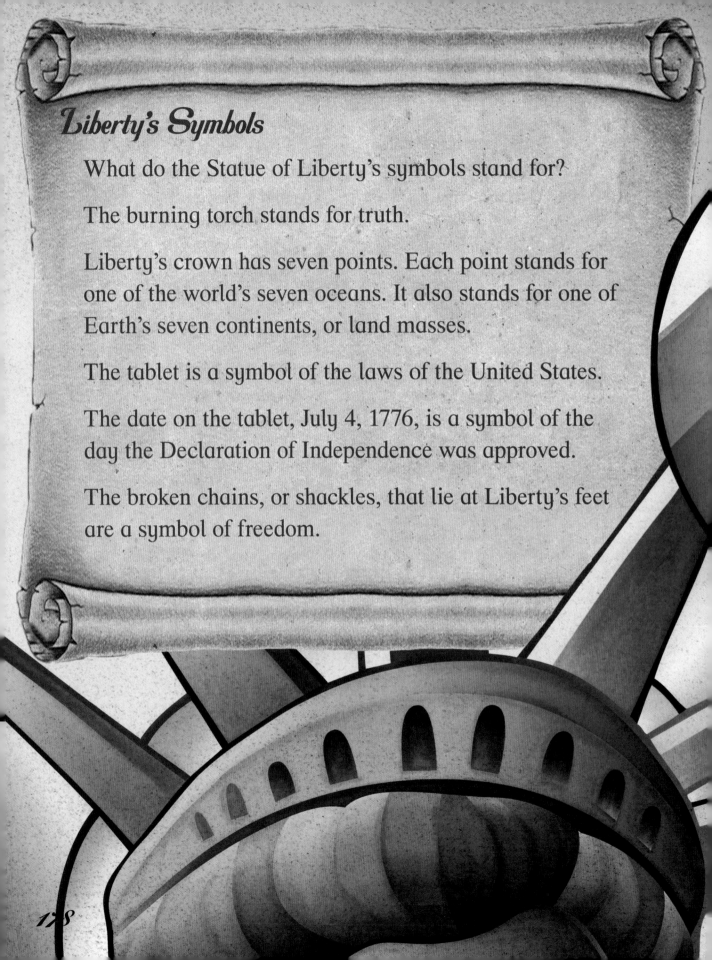

## Liberty's Symbols

What do the Statue of Liberty's symbols stand for?

The burning torch stands for truth.

Liberty's crown has seven points. Each point stands for one of the world's seven oceans. It also stands for one of Earth's seven continents, or land masses.

The tablet is a symbol of the laws of the United States.

The date on the tablet, July 4, 1776, is a symbol of the day the Declaration of Independence was approved.

The broken chains, or shackles, that lie at Liberty's feet are a symbol of freedom.

JULY
IV
MDCCLXXVI

179

The Statue of Liberty is much more than a pretty face. She stands for one of the United States' greatest gifts: freedom! Maybe you can come to New York City soon and visit us. We look forward to seeing you!

# Statue of Liberty Facts

The Statue of Liberty stands on Liberty Island in New York Harbor. Visitors can reach her only by ferry, a special kind of boat.

It took nearly 30 years for the Statue of Liberty's copper to oxidize, or turn from reddish brown to green.

There are 354 stairs from the bottom of the pedestal to the Statue of Liberty's crown.

The Statue of Liberty

The poem "The New Colossus," by American poet Emma Lazarus, was inscribed at the base of the Statue of Liberty in 1903. It contains these now-famous words: "Give me your tired, your poor, / Your huddled masses yearning to breathe free, / The wretched refuse of your teeming shore. / Send these, the homeless, tempest-tost, to me, / I lift my lamp beside the golden door!"

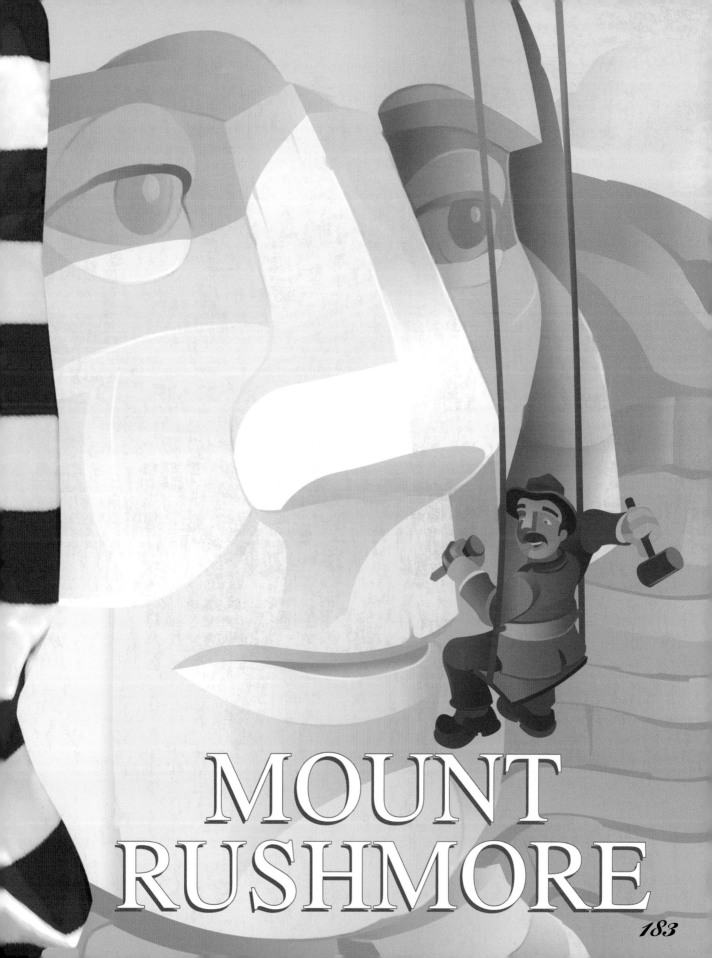

# MOUNT RUSHMORE

Welcome to Mount Rushmore National Memorial! I'm William, a park ranger here. Mount Rushmore is a beautiful symbol of freedom and democracy in the United States. Let's learn its history.

The Lakota Sioux originally called Mount Rushmore "Six Grandfathers" before it was renamed.

# Rushmore

Mount Rushmore is located in the Black Hills of South Dakota. While exploring in 1885, New York lawyer Charles E. Rushmore asked what the mountain was called. His guide suggested they call it Rushmore.

# The Original Plan

In 1923, South Dakota historian Doane Robinson wanted to get people to visit the Black Hills. He imagined giant statues of heroes from the American West. The statues would be part of the rocky peaks in the Black Hills known as the Needles. Robinson thought Americans would travel to see the figures from U.S. history. In the beginning, his idea had nothing to do with Mount Rushmore. That would soon change.

Robinson wanted the face of Red Cloud to be carved into one of the Needles. Red Cloud was a successful Lakota leader from the mid-1800s.

But first, Robinson needed to find an artist with a grand vision.

187

# The Sculptor

In August of 1924, sculptor Gutzon Borglum received a letter. In it, Robinson asked Borglum if he would like to make a "heroic sculpture of unusual character." Within a month, Borglum traveled to South Dakota to meet Robinson.

Borglum imagined carving figures from U.S. history. He drew sketches of his plans. Robinson agreed. But when Borglum checked the location, plans changed. The Needles were too weak to withstand the carving of large sculptures.

Some people did not want the Needles to be carved at all. They believed the natural rock should be left alone.

# A Better Location

Borglum decided Mount Rushmore, just northeast of the Needles, was the best location for the monument. The granite there was strong enough for the work ahead. Mount Rushmore had one of the highest peaks in the Black Hills area. It also stayed well lit throughout most of the day.

"American history shall march along that skyline," Borglum said.

The granite on Mount Rushmore erodes, or wears away, only 1 inch (2.5 centimeters) every 10,000 years.

# The Four Presidents

Borglum wanted to carve the faces of four U.S. presidents into Mount Rushmore. He chose George Washington, the first U.S. president. He also chose Thomas Jefferson, the third U.S. president. Jefferson wrote most of the Declaration of Independence in 1776.

George Washington

Thomas Jefferson

Theodore Roosevelt, the 26th U.S. president, was chosen because of his efforts to complete the Panama Canal. Borglum also chose Abraham Lincoln, the 16th U.S. president. Lincoln led the United States through the Civil War (1861–1865) and started the process that would end slavery in the nation.

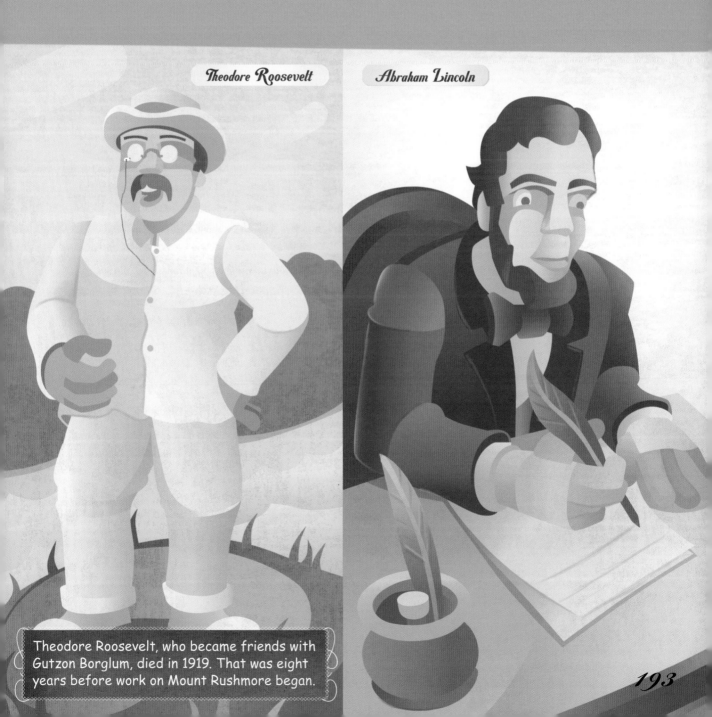

Theodore Roosevelt

Abraham Lincoln

Theodore Roosevelt, who became friends with Gutzon Borglum, died in 1919. That was eight years before work on Mount Rushmore began.

# Kaboom!

After years of planning, the carving of Washington's face began on October 4, 1927. Dynamite was used to clear rock away from the mountain until just a layer of granite remained.

About 450,000 tons (405,000 metric tons) of rock were blasted from the mountainside. Today, the pieces are still scattered below the carved faces.

The last layer of rock was worked away using a process called honeycombing. Workers drilled holes 1 to 6 inches (2.5 to 15.2 cm) deep and about 1 inch (2.5 cm) apart. Then they shaped the stone using very sharp hand tools.

# Mountain Carvers

Although Borglum was a famous sculptor, he didn't carve the faces of Mount Rushmore. Instead, crews of men were hired to shape the rock.

The work was often difficult. The summer sun made the granite very hot to work with. During winter, the men worked until severe cold forced them to stop.

More than 400 people worked on Mount Rushmore.

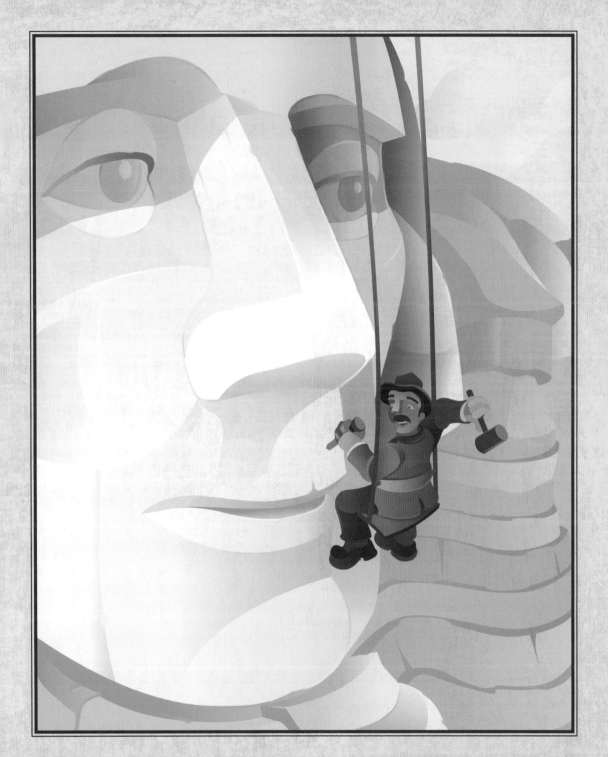

Workers also faced many dangers. They had to use dynamite. At times, they dangled from the mountainside while using tools that weighed nearly 60 pounds (27 kilograms)! The work was tough and dangerous, but the pay was good at the time. A carver was paid $1.25 an hour.

# Dedication

The sculpture of George Washington was dedicated on July 4, 1930. That was two years and nine months after work on Mount Rushmore began.

Women from Rapid City, South Dakota, sewed a giant flag to cover Washington's face until it was revealed at the dedication. It measured 39 feet (11.9 meters) by 70 feet (21.4 m)!

Thomas Jefferson's sculpted face was dedicated in August 1936. President Franklin Roosevelt was in attendance. On September 17, 1937, the sculpture of Abraham Lincoln's face was dedicated. The date marked the 150th anniversary of the U.S. Constitution. Theodore Roosevelt's sculpted face was dedicated on July 2, 1939.

# Looking Over the Land

In March of 1941, Gutzon Borglum died. His son, Lincoln, was asked to oversee the work on Mount Rushmore.

Because money ran out, work on Mount Rushmore ended on October 31, 1941. The entire project took 14 years and cost nearly $1 million to complete. Despite the dangerous work, not one worker died during the sculpting of Mount Rushmore.

Each of the Mount Rushmore faces is more than three times taller than the Statue of Liberty's face. Each president's face is 60 feet (18.3 m) tall. The Statue of Liberty's face is 17 feet (5.2 m) tall.

201

Mount Rushmore now has nearly 3 million visitors each year. It is a symbol of freedom and democracy. It also reminds us of the American spirit. It proves that not even a mountain can stop a grand vision!

I hope you enjoyed learning about Mount Rushmore's history. Come visit us soon!

## Mount Rushmore Facts

❧ Thomas Jefferson's face was originally carved on George Washington's right. Unfortunately, the rock had cracks in it. After 18 months of carving, the workers blasted Jefferson's face from the mountain with dynamite. Then they carved his face on Washington's left.

❧ Abraham Lincoln's head was never completed. Money ran out for the project, because the U.S. government was sending money to England to help it fight in World War II (1939–1945).

Mount Rushmore

# Glossary

**ambassadors** — the highest ranking people chosen to represent their country while visiting another country

**approved** — given the OK

**architect** — a person who plans what new buildings will look like and decides how the rooms will fit together

**Benjamin Franklin** — an American inventor, author, and Founding Father (a signer of the Constitution)

**Cabinet Room** — the room where the president meets with the Cabinet, the leaders of the different departments (such as agriculture or finance) in the U.S. government

**cartoonist** — a person who draws cartoons

**Civil War (1861-1865)** — the battle between states in the North and South that led to the end of slavery in the United States

**clapper** — the metal tongue inside a bell

**colonies** — lands away from home that are controlled by the homeland, such as the American colonies of Great Britain

**colonists** — people living in a colony or a land that is newly settled

**column** — a tall, narrow structure that supports a building

**commissioners** — a person in a group that is responsible for a special task

**committee** — a group of people chosen for a special task

**Congress** — the group of people in the U.S. government who make laws

**Constitution** — the basic rules of the U.S. government

**copper** — a kind of metal

**Declaration of Independence** — a document written by Thomas Jefferson in 1776; it declares the United States a free and independent country and says that every U.S. citizen has rights that the government should protect

**dedication** — a ceremony that sets apart a building or structure for a special purpose

**democracy** — a form of government with equal rights and privileges

**design** — to make something with a plan in mind

**Fort McHenry** — a fort in Baltimore, Maryland, that successfully defended Baltimore Harbor from the British navy in the War of 1812

**funds** — money

**granite** — a hard, gray type of rock

**immigrants** — people who come to a new country to live

**Lakota Sioux** — a Native American tribe from North and South Dakota

**memorial** — something that helps people remember an important person or event

**molds** — forms that give something a special shape

**mural** — a painting on a wall

**national anthem** — a country's special patriotic song

**official** — approved by the government

**patriotism** — love for one's own country

**pavilion** — a roofed shelter

**pedestal** — a base for something to stand on

**platform** — a raised, flat surface

**pyramid** — an object with four triangle-shaped sides that meet at a point on top

**Revolutionary War** — (1775-1783) American fight for freedom from British rule

**seal** — a mark or stamp

**Secret Service agent** — a person whose main job is to protect the president

**shield** — a piece of armor used to protect the body from attack

**Situation Room** — the room where the president meets with members of his or her staff to talk about urgent matters

**slavery** — the practice of owning other people called slaves

**slaves** — people who are owned by other people and are not free

**staff** — a group of people who work together for a common goal

**symbol** — an object that stands for something else

**toll** — the sound of a ringing bell

**U.S. Constitution** — the plan for how the U.S. government works

**veterans** — people who have served in the armed forces, such as the Army

**War of 1812** — (1812–1815) a war between the United States and Great Britain over unfair British control of shipping; often called the "Second War of Independence"

**World War I** — (1914–1918) the war between the Central Powers (Germany, Austria-Hungary, and Turkey) and the Allied Powers (mainly France, Great Britain, Russia, Italy, Japan, and the United States)

**World War II** — (1939–1945) a war in which the United States, France, Great Britain, the Soviet Union, and other allied nations defeated Germany, Italy, and Japan. World War II started when Germany invaded Poland. It ended with the surrender of Germany and Japan.

**yoke** — a thick piece of wood from which a bell hangs

# Index

Editors: Jill Kalz, Shelly Lyons, Nick Healy and Kay Olson
Designers: Abbey Fitzgerald, Tracy Davies and Lori Bye
Art Directors: Keith Griffin and Nathan Gassman
Page Production: Jane Klenk
Media Researcher: Marcie Spence

The illustrations in this book were created digitally.

Photo credits: Shutterstock, 27 (top); Library of Congress, 27 (middle and bottom), 93 (both),
137 (bottom); Shutterstock/Racheal Grazias, 49; Shutterstock/Gualberto Becerra, 71 (right);
Shutterstock/Eugene Moerman, 115; Photodisc, 137; Shutterstock/Jeremy R. Smith, 159;
Shutterstock/ Janes Kingman, 181; Shutterstock/Mike Liu, 203.

Picture Window Books
A Capstone Imprint
151 Good Counsel Drive
P.O. Box 669
Mankato, MN 56002
www.capstonepub.com

Printed in the United States of America in North Mankato, Minnesota.
032010
005710

All books published by Picture Window Books
are manufactured with paper containing at least
10 percent post-consumer waste.

Library of Congress Cataloging-in-Publication Data
Celebrate America: A Guide to America's Greatest Symbols / by
Mary Firestone ... [et al.] ; illustrations by Matthew Skeens.
    p. cm. — (American symbols)
  Includes index.
  ISBN 978-1-4048-6170-1 (pbk.)
 1. National monuments—United States—Juvenile literature.
2. Historic sites—United States—Juvenile literature. 3. Emblems,
National—United States—Juvenile literature. 4. Signs and
symbols—United States—Juvenile literature. I. Firestone, Mary. II.
Skeens, Matthew.
  E159.A387 2010
  973—dc22                          2009046999